# *Hope*
## FOR A
# WOMAN'S
# HEART

**CHRISTIAN ART**
**PUBLISHERS**

# Contents

# One

# Be
# *Picture Perfect*

"A woman views the world
through the windows of her soul
and then draws pictures of
things, experiences and people
to hang on the wall of
remembrance in her heart."

*Y*ou witness the beauty of a flower,
experience the peace of a sunset and
feel emotions intensely ...

because you are a woman.

*Y*ou view the world through the windows of your soul
and then draw pictures of things, experiences and
people to hang on the wall of remembrance in your heart.

*W*hat does the painting of your life look like? How
do other people experience you when they interact
with you? Do they see a barren wilderness, because your soul so
desperately craves the living water? Has the hurt of life drawn
you as a bitter and lonely human ruin?

Or do others experience that the craggy mountains and
dark dungeons you have survived have colored you brightly
and given you exceptional beauty? Is the picture of your life an
inspiring wild flower, a vase of joyful sunflowers or a murmuring
mountain stream?

*M*aybe we will never really know how other people experience us, but we can strive to live every day in a breathtakingly beautiful way!

## Remember:

- Your Savior has cleansed the canvas of your life to pure white. Today you can start afresh, irrespective of the scenes of all your yesterdays!

- Confidently place your life in the perfect Artist's hand. You'll be amazed at the beauty He is able to create.

- God's Word offers a palette of the most beautiful colors of wisdom to paint your life's picture. Dip the paintbrush of your heart deep into the colorful abundance of the Bible.

*If you live with Him, your life will be a living blessing, framed by the beauty of His love.*

Thank You, Artist of my heart,
that You have painted my life over again
and that You spoil me
with so much beauty.

Draw the painting of my soul
every day to the perfection
of Your image so that others
may see something of Your beauty
and Your holiness in me …
so that others would want to know You more.

*Amen.*

# Do You Know the Difference?

*I*magine the following two scenes: In one, a heap of stones covers the broken body of a woman. The blood from her wounds has stained the soil a cruel red. You witness her groaning body turning under the constant assault of the stoning ...

*T*hen you see another scene: The same woman is standing amongst a group of men – each with a stone in the hand – ready to condemn her to death. This scene, however, turns out differently. Jesus is there. You see Him calmly talking to the men, and then you watch as they put down the stones and disappear one by one from the scene. The once frightened and uncertain woman walks away filled with joy. The Son of God has saved her life.*

*W*hen Christ came to the earth, the scenes of our lives changed dramatically. With ONE single act, He removed the stones of sin that were heaped upon us. Through believing in Him we can live each day as joyful, jubilant women!

"Dearest woman, you can live in freedom and hope. I have long forgotten all your stones of sin!" – Your Savior

* John 8:1-11

# Two

# Replenished by God's *Peace*

When you have nothing left within yourself …
that is sometimes the most exhilarating place to be.

*W*orrying drains you bit by bit from the inside. It restricts your throat, knots your stomach, and carves a frown on your forehead. And while the problems you face start resembling Mount Everest, your breathing becomes more and more shallow … and you feel utterly weary.

It is sad that we who are God's children and know that we should place our lives in His hands don't manage to do this during times of intense distress. We pray, but we still struggle forth on our own; we read God's promises in the Scriptures, but we don't really lay claim to these promises. We pray without fully believing.

*I*f you are experiencing these feelings, the time has arrived for your eyes to once again see – really see – your Father approaching you with outstretched arms, ready to embrace you. Find quiet there, against His breast, and experience how He holds you to His heart and enfolds you in His all-encompassing care. Experience how His mighty hand of mercy envelops your entire being and enfolds you like a precious pearl.

Imagine this picture, and then take a deep breath while you surrender all your concerns to Him unconditionally.

Experience how He starts replenishing you bit by bit with His peace.

*A*nxious times are distressing. And yet these times can constitute some of the most exhilarating seasons of our lives. During these times, we realize that we don't have all the solutions and God has the opportunity to reveal His greatness to us. This once again fills the vessels of our faith.

# During Impossible Times …
## God Makes it Possible!

*S*he was a single parent. She lived a life of poverty and deprivation, but her heart was pure. Therefore, the widow of Zarephath had no problem using her last oil and flour to bake Elijah a small cake of bread.*

And just then – when her jars and jugs were totally empty – the miracle occurred. In the days following the incident, her jars and jugs simply stayed full day after day, no matter how much oil and flour she used.

*B*ut the miracle became even greater. Later, when her son died, God raised him from the dead, and we bear witness to how she seized life with renewed faith.

*S*ometimes God takes us to a place in our lives where we are nothing … can do nothing … in order that He may show us who He really is and what He can really do.

* 1 Kings 17:8-24

13

Sometimes, Lord, the constant struggle
with life drains my heart
and leaves me discouraged
about where I should turn tomorrow.

Then … in my emptiness
You become my Only God.
Then I once again realize:
You never forsake empty vessels.
In Your own time and way
You fill the lives
of Your faithful children
once again with exciting answers,
with solutions far greater
than we can imagine!

Today, dear Father, I trust You in this!

*Amen.*

Yes, You came when

I called; You told me,

"Do not fear."

Lam. 3:57

# Three

# Forgiveness Sets You *Free*

Forgiving is sometimes extremely difficult, and yet the result is **blissfully liberating!**

We live in a broken world each day as imperfect people who do not always behave justly, reasonably or in good faith. Therefore, the razor-sharp words and back-stabbing actions of people cut the hearts of others to shreds.

It is an unavoidable reality that we may sometimes have just cause to feel angry, aggrieved or hurt. We do, however, have a choice whether we remain angry and bitter! Every time someone offends or hurts us, we have a choice. We can choose to nurture our resentment and bitterness, or we can choose to share our forgiveness unconditionally.

The fact remains that every one of us breaks our Father's heart in different ways throughout our lives. Every one of us constantly gives Him good reason to be angry with us and disappointed in us.

And yet, despite the daggers with which we pierce His heart, God offers us the liberating forgiveness of the cross!

*A*s soon as we can succeed in setting others free with the unconditional forgiveness of our Lord, we will experience our heavy-laden hearts becoming as light as feathers and the destructive power of bitterness and resentment making way for true peace. Yes, when the glory of divine forgiveness truly flows through our hearts, the impurities of non-forgiveness will naturally disappear from our lives … leaving only love.

*M*aybe the time has come to choose your own freedom: to give those people you simply cannot forgive to God and then declare: "Lord, today I choose to exchange my oppressing, bitter heart for one that is truly free, one that is filled with love."

# Lord Jesus,

You know how easily we
trample on one another's hearts
and how difficult it then is
to share true forgiveness.
I am tired of harboring my
own angry and bitter heart, Father.

Please let Your forgiving love flow
so powerfully through me today
that each chamber of my heart
is purified like newly-fallen snow.
Yes, Father, cleanse me so that
Your love can freely flow through me
and I can be a living channel
of Your type of forgiving love,
so that Your love can flourish.

# Amen.

## Forgiving Love

They tormented Jesus so cruelly, pressing the crown of thorns down into His head and forcefully driving the nails into His hands and feet. Their behavior was so brutal – completely unjustified. We would undoubtedly call it punishable. And yet we hear Jesus immediately petitioning the Father to forgive them and not to punish them.

You and I daily drive nails into our Lord's heart – sometimes unintentionally, other times fully conscious of what we are doing. And every time, the Son intercedes on our behalf: "Father, forgive her, for she does not realize what she is doing."*

May our gratitude for His absolute forgiveness and love compel us every day to forgive over and over … and over again.

* Luke 23:34 (adapted)

# Four

# A Heavenly Privilege

Motherhood is a **heavenly privilege.** But fulfilling this role is a challenge you can only tackle from your knees!

$\mathcal{M}$otherhood is an enormous joy. But being a mother is definitely not always easy. Raising (innocent!) bundles to adulthood requires a great amount of energy, wisdom and patience. And the older our children get, the more energy, wisdom and patience we need.

And just when we start to think that the difficult part of motherhood is over, we have to set our little chicks, whom we have lovingly nurtured, free to fly into the world. It is then that we mother eagles realize: **Our children are merely lent to us for a short while.**

$\mathcal{M}$oses' mother was one of those women in the Bible with exceptional courage. In her effort to save her baby boy from the murderous campaign of the Egyptians, she wove a basket, covered it with impermeable tar and pitch, put the baby in it and hid him among the reeds. Pharaoh's daughter found him and arranged with Moses' mother to raise the child and then bring him to the palace.

In Exodus 2, we read how Moses' mother took care of him and then "gave" him to the princess at the agreed time. Imagine how much courage she needed for this part of the agreement! Three things are essential to ensure successful motherhood: The unbreakable basket of our specially-woven love, our impermeable example, and the willingness to release our children among the reeds of life … so that they can live their own lives.

# Pray for the necessary courage to have all three of these things.

Perfect Father,
I can only be a mother through You.
Only with Your help
am I able to give life
and help to form a person.

Every single day, please be
my Guide and Counselor,
my Stronghold and Strength.
Yes, shape my thoughts, words and actions
so that I may be the best mother I can be
through You.
*Amen.*

The Lord is my
strength and shield.
I trust Him with all
my heart.
He helps me,
and my heart is filled
with joy.

Ps. 28:7

# Five

# *Listen!*
## God Is Whispering

God speaks to His children in different ways …
sometimes as clear as a bell, and at other times by
means of a soft whispering ...

Do you sometimes struggle to hear God's voice? Do you occasionally feel that He is a distant God, and do you then wonder whether He really loves you? Many a child of faith and even biblical champions of faith have experienced times when they feel abandoned.

The good news is that God has not turned His back on you. He loves you far too much to do that! Usually it is merely circumstances beyond your control or even your innermost being that has estranged you from Him. During times like these, you should ask yourself:

- Have I been too busy lately to talk to God?
- Have I allowed sin and feelings of guilt to build a wall between us?
- Has the noise of the world deafened me to His voice?

*E*lijah, one of the great prophets, also experienced a wilderness time during his life. Exhausted and isolated from God and people, he wished to die. And when God appeared to Him once again, it was not in a dramatic way.

In 1 Kings 19, we read that God did not appear to him in the wind, an earthquake or even a fire, but in "the sound of a gentle whisper." Elijah heard God's whisper in the silence.

## Remember ...

- God is never too busy to listen to you and to talk to you. He patiently waits on you with an understanding ear.
- Nothing can separate you from His love. Your forgiving Father hears the repentant heart of His children loud and clear.
- God does not compete against the noise of the world. He does not shout. He whispers when your soul is ready.

*Nothing* can separate you
from God's *love*!

When I become quiet beside You, Lord,
Your glorious presence envelops
my soul with tender peace.
When I am with You,
Your tender love fills my entire being.
When You shelter me,
You whisper new life into my heart.

Being with You
fills me with more joy
than anything else ever can.
Maybe this is because Your presence
fills Your children with so much
unconditional love.
*Amen.*

# Live Again!

*W*inter months have a way of leaving us feeling rather empty, as if the drab surroundings and the cold and leafless branches could freeze out all joy within us.

That is the time when we just want to crawl under a blanket and hide from everyone and everything.

*B*ut winter can be very special. This time can allow you to sit quietly and listen for God's whisper. Take time to frequently sit at the fireplace of God's love during the winter weeks.

Ask Him to dispel the coldness from your heart, brighten the drab around you with His rainbow of mercy and speak His words to you.

"My child,

I miss you. Come and sit beside Me

so that I may tell you how much I love you

and how precious you are to Me."

– Your Father God

# More Than Enough
## *Faith*

*Six*

*L*ord, it is so difficult to do all the things You expect us to do. And we have so little faith. Please increase our faith." Does this sound like the cry of your own heart? Like the doubts you frequently experience? Then you are human. The words of the apostles in Luke 17 have been voiced by many a sincere believer.

*D*espite our attempts to believe unconditionally, we often find that our faith is lacking and that we struggle to grow spiritually. Today, Jesus answers you in the same way He answered the plea for faith uttered by His disciples: "You don't need a lot of faith to do great things for the Lord. A little bit is more than enough. Just use it!" (see Luke 17:6).

# How Can You Believe (More)?

- Love God unconditionally. Love for Him is the root of faith!
- Daily declare your total dependence on Him. His Spirit will come to your rescue in your weakness.
- Open your heart to His voice. His strength will sustain you.
- Nourish your faith with the promises from His Word. He is true to His promises.
- Obey Him. Then all things will work out according to His perfect plan.
- Trust Him under all circumstances. His grace will sustain you.
- See the unseen. He always takes care of you and waits for you at the gates of heaven.

*Saint Augustine said that faith is believing what you don't see. And the result is that you see what you can hardly believe.*

Almighty God,
You enable me to do anything,
You faithfully bless me, sustain me and guide me.
Will You please help me to also believe?

Yes, Lord, take my tiny
mustard-seed faith
and grow it –
branch by branch –
into a leafy tree.
Into a tree that says:
I was planted next to
the Living Waters
and therefore abundant blessings
flow forth from me.

*Amen.*

Believe, grow and
live from the power
of your faith!

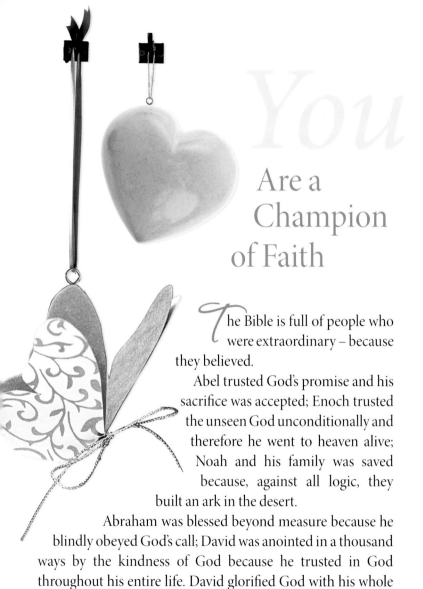

# You
## Are a Champion of Faith

*T*he Bible is full of people who were extraordinary – because they believed.

Abel trusted God's promise and his sacrifice was accepted; Enoch trusted the unseen God unconditionally and therefore he went to heaven alive; Noah and his family was saved because, against all logic, they built an ark in the desert.

Abraham was blessed beyond measure because he blindly obeyed God's call; David was anointed in a thousand ways by the kindness of God because he trusted in God throughout his entire life. David glorified God with his whole life – even when he felt small, showed remorse for his sins, fled in fear and experienced profound joy.

We may be just ordinary people, but when we obey and trust in God, He makes us extraordinary champions of faith who stand in His service.

*W*oman of faith, trust Me with all your heart.

Know that when you lose your way, you will hear

My voice behind you saying:

"This is the way you should go."

Isa. 30:21

# Seven

# Generous *Grace*

Grace recreates people at no cost.

*G*race is simply *given*. Grace takes the useless pieces of our patchwork lives and, without our even asking for it, sews them together to form beautiful, complete pictures.

It takes hearts that have been dragged through the mud and sends them to the heavenly dry cleaners to be washed spotlessly clean, neatly ironed and hung back on the hangers of life.

Grace once again turns the hopeless into people of hope, changes bitterness into forgiveness and transforms the lost into children of eternity. Through grace, a miserable future is transformed into a life of anticipation about tomorrow.

*G*odly grace is not subject to conditions, does not have any expectations, does not set rules and never reproaches. Grace says, "I love you just as you are. You don't have to adhere to any demands; you don't have to first work, give or serve. I give you my forgiveness, acceptance and love while you are who and what you are. I came to sew together the tattered pieces of broken lives to form a heavenly unity."

*G*od's grace is too big to understand, yet it forms the very core of our faith. It is the essence of love, life and eternity with Christ.

*F*ortunately, we don't have to understand the full extent of God's grace before we can accept it. All we need to do is gratefully embrace what is given to us so unconditionally and make it our own.

*H*ave you really allowed the vastness of your Father's grace to sew together the pieces of your life and make you whole? Have you allowed grace to recreate you?

# Lord,

my life is a bunch of
frayed pieces of cloth
that serves no purpose,
makes no sense
and simply cannot be
whole in itself.

Thank You for loving me
as I am.
Thank You that Your grace picks up
the pieces of my life
and then sews them together
to form a meaningful complete life …
transforming me into a new person.

Teach me to cover others
with the tenderness of
my patchwork heart …
with the grace of
my comforting love …
out of gratitude for the
magnitude of Your grace.

# Amen.

# "Not because I deserve it ... "

*I* am so thankful for Paul – the man who unequivocally told us in so many ways the truth concerning salvation in Christ. He convinced us that rules cannot save us, but that we can live as truly liberated people within the sphere of God's glorious grace.

I am so thankful for Christ – the Man who made it possible for us to live as redeemed people forever.

*M* ay we live as obedient and joyous patchwork people, out of gratitude for the undeserved grace of our Father.

Even before He made the world, God loved us and chose us in Christ to be holy and without fault in His eyes. God decided in advance to adopt us into His own family by bringing us to Himself through Jesus Christ.

Eph. 1:4-5

# Eight

# *Immanuel* –
## Our Light, Comfort and Hope

We all know what it feels like when darkness extinguishes the light in our hearts, when the shutters of our souls are drawn and we hide from the penetrating rays of the sun. When we are overcome with grief, shock, pain and depression, we want to run away from the world and everything that reminds us of light.

Sometimes it is necessary to linger in the dark for a while. To consciously experience how darkness envelops us and to embrace it ... as long as, in the midst of our darkness, we still seek the face of the Lord. Because He is there.

Jesus entered into the darkest realms of death in order to walk with us through our dark times today. His light was completely extinguished so that He could be our Light in our darkest hours.

The more you focus on Him in your darkest hours, the more you will see His light. The tighter you hold onto His hand, the more you will be aware of His intense presence, His loving comfort and His tender healing.

In His perfect timing, He will once again open up the windows of your soul and allow His joyful sun to light up your heart. That is when you will realize that He was always with you through your darkness.

Sometimes we have to linger in the dark for a while. Only then can we see the Lord in a different light, get to know Him better and understand that our Immanuel God is indeed our only light, comfort and hope in darkness.

Father,

at times the darkness in my life blinds me.
These are the times when my heart succumbs to
grief, suffering and loneliness;
when I am pain-stricken and defenseless
and struggling to see You.

Enable me to keep focusing on You
until I can clearly see Your greatness.
Until I experience Your grace
once again flooding my life,
the shutters of my soul opening up
and my whole being lighting up.
Until I once again see the Light!

Amen.

## He Cries with You

*J*esus knew how to linger in the dark. When John tells of the death of Lazarus, we read of three occasions* where Jesus was described as sad, grief-stricken and even angry over the death of His friend. He wept with the by-standers because He could actually feel the pain and identify with it.

*I*n your darkest hour, this same Jesus stands beside you and gently enfolds you with His comfort. Yes, He is with you – especially at times like these. You just need to see Him.

God blesses those who patiently endure testing and temptation.

James 1:12

* John 11:33, 35, 38

# Nine

# Be *With* Him

The Holy Spirit wants to spoil you with His presence every day.

The Spirit of God has a whole treasure chest of blessings in store for us every day.

He is there every moment of every day, ready to work in us, through us and for us – and then we choose not to receive it! Yes, it is so easy not to hear Him because He is simply not a priority in our lives, because we are too busy or too scared to hear what He wants to say to us! And consequently we miss out on a glorious share of God's grace.

When we allow the Spirit to work within us, our fear is transformed into trust, our helplessness into deliverance, our confusion into truth and our despair into faith and new hope. Our self-centered view of life will be transformed into a purpose-driven life: a life in which we strive to share His love, power and peace with others.

But spending time with the Spirit is more than an act of will. It means choosing to become silent and practice the art of really listening. It requires that you come to a halt somewhere in your busy day, seek solitude and allow Him to speak to you. It requires that you empty yourself of your own concerns in order to be filled with Him … and in doing so experience fulfillment.

Set aside time for the Spirit and listen expectantly as He speaks to you through the Word, prayer, circumstances, people and your thoughts. You'll be surprised at what He has to say to you.

You'll be even more surprised at what He can achieve through you!

How amazing
that You are at my disposal, Holy Spirit.
That You are there every day
to impart wisdom to me,
to encourage me,
to strengthen me in my weakness
and to fill me with Your peace.

I want to make You a priority,
live intimately with You,
silently listen to You,
and expectantly hear what You have to say.
I want to experience You powerfully working
in, through, for,
and even in spite of me.

*Amen.*

# The True Light

The Spirit has a way of radically directing and changing people's lives. Just like Paul's life. Acts tells us how Saul (later Paul) frantically persecuted the Christians until the Spirit powerfully stopped him in his tracks, closed his eyes to the darkness and revealed the true Light to him.

Thereafter, he was an unstoppable man of God – an exemplary icon of faith.*

Just imagine what the Spirit of God is able to do through you!

I pray that God, the source of hope, will fill you completely with joy and peace because you trust in Him. Then you will overflow with confident hope through the power of the Holy Spirit.

Rom. 15:13

* Acts 9

# Ten

# Really Listening

Prayer is so much more than talking.
It is standing in awe of God's embracing love.
It is knowing that He is with you.

We have become experts at talking. Talking to one another, on our cell phones, over the Internet and in our prayers. We do this talking thing so well that we are no longer able to listen. Therefore, we often fail to hear one another's hearts and miss the real emotions behind the words we speak. Even worse, we have become deaf to the whisper of God's voice.

Listening is an art we should practice every day. Real listening requires that we forget about ourselves and all the words in our minds and tune in to those who are talking to us. When we start practicing being silent and listening so that our conversational partner's words really make sense to us, something starts happening.

Our hearts become one. We become soulmates.

*W*e must do the same with God. We must tune in to Him. When it is our sincere desire *to hear* the Father's voice, we will initially struggle with all the noise within us. That is when the purging process must begin. We must learn to let go of every one of our thoughts … until we are quiet enough to really take in the word God has for us and make it our own.

*L*et us once again practice the art of really listening. We may just be surprised at what we hear – maybe even for the first time.

Lord, I talk far too much!
Consequently I have lost the ability
to listen attentively.

Empty me of myself for a change;
so that I can hear again.
Truly hear what others want to say to me;
Better understand Your world and Your people
and possibly even love them more.

Place me somewhere every day
where I may be quiet enough
to listen to Your voice,
take in Your presence,
hear how much You really love me
and then realize
that You have always listened!

*Amen.*

# Delight in God

Prayer was never an incidental duty to Jesus. He intentionally set aside time to talk to His Father. Often He would actively seek the Father early in the morning before the voices of the crowds started filling His world (see Mark 1:35). Because He made time to listen to His Father, He could truly hear the hearts of people. He was able to understand, to really love and to live life to the fullest.

May you and I daily practice emptying ourselves so that we can be filled with that which is really important. May He grant us the grace to close our mouths and open our ears.

The Lord says, "I will rescue those who love Me.
I will protect those who trust in My name.
When they call on Me, I will answer."

Ps. 91:14-15

# Eleven

# Heavenly *Love*...
# Glorious Aroma

Heavenly love can never be concealed,
especially since its glorious aroma
spreads so easily …

*A*t times love is the overwhelming sweetness of jasmine, and sometimes it's the comfort of freshly percolated coffee or even the peaceful scent of the sea.

In the same way, some people brim over with generous love. Their entire being proclaims: "You are welcome in my heart. Kick off your shoes and just be yourself. Stay a while with me so that my generous love can rub off on you. I want to shed some light when the way before you is dark, offer some shade when the bright rays of life are scorching, or provide a bundle of hope to make your own cozy fire."

Because you feel safe and secure with these people, you want to bask in their presence, you want to linger a while with them. Spend some time away and it won't be long before you need to seek their presence again.

*O*ur heavenly Father wants us to be people who emit a heavenly aroma – something we can only achieve when we allow Him to renew us every day and when His Spirit fills us to overflowing.

Only God can transform ordinary, fallible and heartless people into sincere, love-driven people. Only He can sow a share of His unconditional mercy in our hearts so that we are able to spread the wonder of godly love without limits.

*L*et us pray every day for the aroma of our lives to waft into our world so that our lives may profess: "Welcome into my life. Welcome to love."

Spirit of God,
out of my own I am not capable of love.
Because there is too much of me
and too little of You.

However, with Your kind of love
I can lovingly satisfy
the thirst of others,
offer the food of compassion
to hungry souls
and impart tender peace
to a restless heart.

Void me of myself completely
so that I may be filled with You.
For then, O Lord,
the aroma of Your love
can freely spread forth from me.

*Amen.*

# His Precious Love

The disciples were exhausted after an unsuccessful night of fishing. Fortunately, the Man on the shore suggested that they cast their nets on the other side of the boat and, consequently, they brought home a huge catch. But now they were famished! So the Man invited them to join Him at His cozy fire with these words: "Come and have some breakfast" (John 21:12).

Only after He had broken the bread and handed it to them with the fish did they realize that it was their Master standing before them. He had, like so many times before, spoiled them with His loving kindness.

Your Father frequently calls you to His fire of mercy and then says, "Come and eat from My hand. Come and feed from My presence. Then go and spread My love into your world."

Our lives are a Christ-like fragrance rising up to God. But this fragrance is perceived differently by those who are being saved and by those who are perishing.

2 Cor. 2:15

# Twelve

# Spiritual Growth –
## Your Choice

Growing spiritually is a faith-expanding and
life-changing choice you can make every day.

God will gladly share Himself with you if you choose to
know Him and He will enable you– through His Spirit
and His Scriptures – to become more and more like Him every
day while growing in faith.

But because you are human, you have a natural tendency
to try and get by without God, which leads to spiritual
deterioration. Spiritual growth can never merely be a hobby;
on the contrary, spiritual growth requires giving something of
yourself. It requires that you listen to what the Word has to say
to you and that you try your best to do God's will in your daily
life.

Therefore, you have to remain so close to your Father
throughout the day that you spontaneously flee from the
negative and focus on the holy and good. Growing spiritually
implies that you get to know God better and that you experience
more of His grace every day.

*Choose*

Every day choose to grow your roots deeper in faith by reaching down to the living water of His Word.

Be strengthened by the powerful nourishment of the Spirit and grow upward toward the Light: *His* Light that will help you grow strong and stand firm.

Lord, on my own
I cannot grow spiritually.
My natural being is far too
prone to evil.
Therefore, I want to live so intimately
with You that what I learn from You …
what You are …
truly lives through me.

Please feed me daily with
Your Word and Your truth
until it fills my mind,
determines my lifestyle,
and enables me to
truly live in Your love.
*Amen.*

# Living Your Faith

*P*eter is known as the impertinent disciple of Jesus. This was the man who could boldly talk and make promises, but then denied Jesus three times when He was at His most defenseless.

However, the letters that Peter wrote later on tell the story of a man who grew spiritually. Gradually, his knowledge of faith began to dictate his lifestyle to such an extent that he was prepared to live unashamedly for God every day … and eventually to die for Him.

*T*oday this man of faith is saying to you: Because we really know Him, His divine power has instilled in us everything we need to live intimately with Him (see 2 Pet.1:3). Be assured today: You, too, can continue to grow spiritually and make your faith a living practice every day.

*Make every effort to respond to God's promises.*
*Supplement your faith with a generous provision of moral*
*excellence, and moral excellence with knowledge.*
*2 Pet. 1:5*

# Thirteen

# Let *Joy* Surprise You

### Sometimes we have to work to make joy happen.

One can hardly believe that the renowned Christian author, C. S. Lewis, once was a self-professed atheist. During that time in his life, his doctoral writings were described as cynical and gloomy. How very different his writings became once he repented and believed in the Savior! And it is significant that his first book after his conversion was titled *Surprised by Joy*. With God, he experienced true joy for the first time.

If you were to write a book about your life, what would

the title be? Would it reveal something about hope, courage, joy and expectation? Or would the topics covered between the pages mostly revolve around your suffering and pain, your aches and trials … your cheerless existence?

*M*aybe you have good reason to have a gloomy view of life. And yet as children of God, we are called to think differently about life:

- You are cherished! Your loving Father tenderly watches over you and will take care of you every day of your existence.
- You are free! Christ has already forgiven you, so there is no reason whatsoever for you to keep on punishing yourself over your own brokenness.
- You are not alone! The comforting Holy Spirit is with you every moment to help you write the story of your life.

*A*sk the Spirit to surprise you with joy every day. Pray that the Light will brighten your world. Know that the great Provider will always bless your life with joy and peace. Therefore, live today with joyful expectation. Then … be surprised by joy!

What a privilege, dear God,
that You are the Author of my life!
How comforting
that You watch over me unceasingly,
that I may be Your redeemed child
and that You are with me 24/7.

Please write my name in the Book of Life
with the ink of Your grace
so that the story of my life
will relate a tale of
joy, expectation
and eternal hope.

*Amen.*

# Never Abandoned

Three wooden crosses silhouetted sharply against the horizon. Their Master, the One they loved so much, the Man who comforted, guided and instructed them for years, had been crucified. *

Lost, abandoned and confused, these women whom Jesus loved dearly were standing alone and crying. Dismayed, they had to watch their Friend – their Lord – die on the cross! Fortunately, we will never again see Christ crucified. And yet many women today still feel lost and abandoned. Many are eagerly seeking something. They do not know that only in the Savior will they find the joy they seek.

We look forward to eternity with our Savior, but in the meantime He expects us to look beyond the cross, the grave and the ascension clouds. The joy He promises can be our reality today. We are not abandoned; we are His! That should give us joy indeed!

For our present troubles are small and won't
last very long. Yet they produce for us a glory that vastly
outweighs them and will last forever!

2 Cor. 4:17

*John 19:25

# Fourteen

# A *Journey* without Dead Ends

God's plan has no dead ends.
His map for our lives comprises only
roads that lead to new life.

We all know the feeling of "What next?" Like when we are faced with big decisions; or when things don't make sense to us anymore; or when we wonder how we are to gather the shattered pieces of our lives and put them back together again. Sometimes our dead ends are economic pressures; at other times they may be bumpy relationships. Sometimes the dead ends cause us to wander aimlessly in our own world.

During times like these, it is easy to become estranged from God. We wonder whether He understands how our lost hearts feel. We feel guilty that we don't always stick to the "narrow path." We wonder as we wander. And yet, it is in those "lost" times that we need to seek His guidance more than ever. We need to pour out our confusion at His feet and unashamedly ask, "Lord, I don't know which way to go! Please show me the way."

When we surrender to God in total dependence, we will hear His whispering voice, "My child, you are not at a dead end; you have merely taken a temporary detour. Don't allow your view to be obstructed by the T-junction in front of you. Look to the left and to the right so that you may see that I have brought you to a halt in order for you to take a new direction.

My plan for you is full of opportunities, interesting possibilities, exciting challenges and a life that will last forever. Stand up and follow Me so that I may show you the path ahead."

Lord, today I realize that
You are with me on my way,
and that every bit of my life
is part of Your **perfect plan.**
On this pilgrimage there will always be
answers, solutions and
the right outcome.

Open my eyes to Your way and Your truth
so that I may hear Your voice,
follow the right path
and arrive safely at my
heavenly home.

*Amen.*

# Expect a Surprise!

First Samuel 13 to 16 tells a dead-end tale. At least that's what it looks like when we learn of King Saul's unfaithfulness to the Lord and how God decided to end his reign immediately. The prophet Samuel soon realized that God already had another plan in mind when He sent him to go and identify another king.

After Samuel had seen seven potential candidates and received a "no" from God every time, the innocent shepherd boy, David, appeared before him. It was then that the Lord said, "This is the one; anoint him" (1 Sam. 16:12). The boy, fresh from watching his sheep, found himself anointed by oil to one day become a great king of Israel.

"I am the Lord your God, who teaches you
what is good for you and leads you
along the paths you should follow."

Isa. 48:17

# Fifteen

# Be Good to *Yourself*

Spoiling your soul
is something you can do …
may do … have to do every day.

Being spoiled is one of those perks of being a child. Those unexpected cookies in the lunch box, Mom snugly tucking you in before her last goodnight kiss, carefree times of fun and laughter, lazy summer days … or even something as insignificant as a box of sugar candy.

Now we are all grown up. And we are the ones who spoil everyone else … except ourselves! Decide to be good to yourself more often by finding time for some colorful "sugar candy" moments for your soul:

- **Red:** Experience anew how much God and others love you. Cherish that realization like a bright red heart.
- **Pink:** Write a love letter to yourself (yes, yourself!) to remind you why you are a special woman.
- **Green:** Ask the Spirit to help you continually grow to be more and more like Christ.

- **Blue:** Lie down in the grass and look at the sky. Thank God for the beauty of His awesome creation.
- **Orange:** Watch the sun rise. Allow the orange glow of a new day to fill your heart with positive expectations, hope and courage.
- **Purple and white:** Gather some flowers and, as you take in their fresh scent, remember that your Father ceaselessly takes care of you – just like He takes care of every flower in the field.
- **Black and brown:** Don't fret about the dark moments that bring aches to your heart. Remember that even those moments have a purpose, and that God will use them for His great glory.

Your soul needs special times of nurturing. Even if you are all grown up! So spoil yourself a little …

Lord Jesus,

You know every colorful part of my life,
but You also know about
the dull colorless parts.

Yes, You spoil me every day
with Your brightly colored love
that I so thoroughly enjoy.

Teach me to live like a child again
and experience the joy of
each of Your blessings.
Yes, teach me to once again
live passionately
and find peace in the fact that
You are with me, loving Spirit.

*Amen.*

# A Colorful Woman

Beautiful, intelligent, diplomatic and determined … these words would describe Esther.* That is why she is still one of the most colorful women in the Bible. She did not hesitate to fully enjoy and utilize every aspect of her life as a woman.

Eventually, she single-handedly rescued her people through her own courage and determination.

Esther serves as a role model to us as women of this modern era:

- She nurtured her appearance and took pains with and enjoyed every aspect of her femininity.
- She really cared about other people and was prepared to fight for the greater cause.
- She lived wholeheartedly: Whether she was working or celebrating – she did it with all her heart and soul.

Washington Irving proclaimed that in the heart of a true woman there is a spark of heavenly fire that is dormant in the daylight of prosperity, but lights up and burns brightly in the darkness of adversity.

I have a special selection of blessings for you on the shelves of My heart. Ask, and I will gladly lavish those blessings on you. – Your Father

* Esther 1-10

# When Your *Heart* Is Aching

# Sixteen

When we have a headache, we swallow a tablet; when we have grazed a knee, we stick a bandage over it; when something more serious is wrong in our bodies, we go to a hospital. But when our hearts are broken, we usually don't know what to do.

The ache of a broken heart is simply too big for tablets, bandages or even nurturing care from others. When our hearts are broken, not even a best friend, the most experienced counselor or the greatest heart surgeon can heal the hurt.

They can listen, comfort, offer advice and pour balm into the wounds, but nothing can magically make those deep wounds disappear.

*W*hen your heart is bleeding, there is only one place where you can find relief: at the feet of your Father. When you take the pieces of your broken heart to Him, when you listen quietly to His Word and focus on Him, He will take the brokenness and restore you piece by piece … gradually healing you.

*T*he deeper the wound, the more time you need with Him. The greater the hurt and the more intense the loneliness of your heartache, the richer you will find His grace and His compassionate love to be.

*M*ay you always remember where to go when your heart is aching, and may you gradually experience healing in Him.

Sometimes, Lord, my heart
is too broken to be mended again.
These are the times that I
want to hide myself in a cocoon
so that nobody can come close to me.

In times like these, thank You
for hearing the words I cannot utter
and seeing the hurt I don't want to admit.
Thank You for holding me
in Your tender hands
and carrying me until
my heart is once again ready
to greet the world.

Thank You for being a Healer
to brokenhearted people …
and to me.

*Amen.*

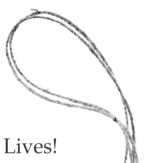

# Live! Because He Lives!

Can you imagine how devastated Mary was when she saw the broken body of her Son on the cross? Imagine how discouraged, helpless and brokenhearted she must have felt that day. Can you imagine how elated she was on the Sunday morning when she received the news that her Son had risen, that He was alive?

In the darkest Fridays of our lives, God is closer than ever to us. He knows how to sustain us until Sunday, until we reach the day of hope.

He has sent me to comfort the brokenhearted.

Isa. 61:1

# Obedience
## to God

# Seventeen

Obedience to God doesn't happen automatically. We are far too human for that.

Children aren't the only ones who have difficulty listening, hearing and doing. We grown-ups often also struggle being unconditionally obedient to the voice, commands and will of our Father. And yet we know that obedience to God is always worth the effort, because then ...

- We live God's plan – His perfect plan! – for our lives.
- We experience a deep feeling of peace, leaving the control of our lives in His capable hands.
- We feel no guilt, knowing that we are faithful to Him, others and ourselves.
- We experience inner joy under all circumstances because we know that He will make all things work for our good in the end.
- We live according to our highest calling, as image-bearers of His glory.

When we love our Father with all our heart and soul, we want to and will obey Him – unconditionally and under all circumstances.

*Let us pray
every day ...*
to love Him enough

to obey Him

**spontaneously.**

Heavenly Father,
today I admit that
I do not always obey You,
that I often follow my own mind,
and live according to my own will.
These are the times that I mess up,
hurt others and break hearts!
Please **forgive me.**

Help me to constantly
hold on to Your hand
so that I may always have
the ability to spontaneously
say "Yes" to Your call.
May my life always **glorify** You
here, now ... forever.

*Amen.*

# Shining in the Shade

Not every one of us is called to proclaim our faith in public or to be leaders. This is one life lesson Miriam had to learn the hard way. Sometimes God placed her on a pedestal and used her dancing and singing talents to influence the people.

But Miriam had to also learn to sometimes shine in the shade of her brother, Moses. She had to learn to support and help another leader with an obedient heart. *

Our Father uses each one of us in His place, time and way. Therefore, we have to be willing to shine wherever He has placed us – even though it may be in the shade. Know and believe that the Father can and will use your unique abilities in His own way. And then do as He says. That is true obedience.

God works in different ways, but it is the same God who does the work in all of us. A spiritual gift is given to each of us so we can help each other.

1 Cor. 12:6-7

* Exod. 15: 20-21; Num. 12

# Eighteen

# You Are the *Crown* of His Creation

*G*od wanted women to be different. That is why He blessed women with true motherly love, hearts that nurture with compassion, unquestionable intuition and the ability to talk and cry – sometimes without reason!

Furthermore He took care to give women a different look. Like the depth of her eyes, the delicate features of her countenance, her soft, well-groomed hands and the engaging curves of her body. After God had created all the beauty of the world, we were His *finale* – the crescendo of our Master's craftsmanship.

*A*s a woman, you are the crown of His creation; therefore, He thinks differently about you. He – the great Artist – has dreamt about you, planned you and meticulously shaped every part of your heart, soul and body to ensure that you can be *you*. That is why He wants you to be mindful of your unique femininity and to appreciate and enjoy it.

*B*ecause God knows the crown of His creation, He also loves you differently. He understands your vulnerability, frailty and typical feminine soul so well and, therefore, takes extra good care of you.

As He did to His precious nation of Israel so many centuries ago, today He is declaring to you, His crowning glory, "I will be … like a refreshing dew from heaven" (Hosea 14:5). May God's tender dew replenish you every day so that you may realize anew how very precious you are to Him.

Father, it is simply incredible to imagine
that I am the crown of Your creation.
Thank You, dear Father,
for my special femininity,
my uniqueness
and the fact that
I am Your precious child.

Dwell in me so that my life
may enrich this world
with a symphony of beauty.

*Amen.*

# Find Your Perfect Self

*E*ve was the perfect woman… when God created her. Unfortunately, because she wanted to be more than God intended her to be, she chose to betray God, humankind and her own being. Henceforth she struggled, and every Eve after her has struggled to regain the perfect balance within herself.

*A*t times, you and I are also Eves. We eagerly search for our inner selves – our own worth and acceptance – because we believe we have to be more than we already are. And in our attempts to be "better," we do one of two things: We run away from ourselves by trying to control everyone around us, or we hide away in our own lonely, uncertain inner world.

*G*od wants each one of us to find happiness, fulfillment and contentment knowing that the blood of His Son has perfected us once again. Let us pray that the Spirit will rid us of our self-imposed inferiority and reveal to us our beauty and value as God's creations.

The Lord delights in you and will claim you as His bride.
God will rejoice over you
as a bridegroom rejoices over his bride.

Isa. 62:4-5

# Nineteen

# Live in the Sunshine

In the beginning the Creator said,
"Let there be light."
Today, thousands of years later,
God still starts every day anew with the world.

It's so wonderful to know that our Lord is truly a God of new creations, that despite what happened yesterday, He starts every day anew with us. He merely requires that every morning we place our hearts in His hands in total dependence, accept His forgiveness, seek His truth and do His will.

Titus 2:14 states that He "gave His life to free us from every kind of sin, to cleanse us, and to make us His very own people, totally committed to doing good deeds." Why would you persist in suffering from a guilty conscience or sit around moping when He has declared that He wants to renew your spirit?

With every new season, God once again proclaims His reforming love: autumn wants us to rid ourselves of our guilt baggage; winter speaks of our Father's warm and cozy love; the bright splashes of spring flowers paint a picture of His restoring grace; the warm summer sun that caresses our bodies declares: Live, my child, because I live!

From now on, every morning when you hear the joyful song of the birds, remember with thanksgiving and excitement:

## My Savior has cleansed me.
## That is why I live!

Sometimes I cannot **believe**
that You are prepared to
recreate me time and again.
Your forgiveness is great!

**Thank You, Lord** of my life,
that You accept me unconditionally
and love me uncondemningly.
Your mercy is all-embracing!

Teach me to live
with a new heart **every day**.
A heart that shows the world
how enormously great Your love is.

*Amen.*

# When small becomes big

To us he is the sneaky little man in the Sycamore tree. Zacchaeus – the tax collector – was a man who was labelled a sinner … until Jesus noticed him (Luke 19).

The moment that the gracious love of Christ beckoned him, this man's life changed irrevocably. From then on, he could love with a new heart.

Still today, God knocks at the door of our hearts with the request that His gracious love should find a home there. And when we allow Him to enter:

- we become blind to the faults of others, because we see their potential.
- we forgive and forget, and let bygones be bygones.
- we show love in practical and dutiful ways in everything we say, do and are.
- we change the people around us for the better.

When Jesus lives in the hearts of His children, love changes small uncertain people into great ones. How great are you?

The faithful love of the Lord never ends!
His mercies never cease. Great is His faithfulness;
His mercies begin afresh each morning.

Lam. 3:22-23

# You Are Beautiful.
## Believe It!

# Twenty

God does not love you
because you are beautiful;
you are beautiful because He loves you.

Who do you see when you look in the mirror? Someone who is filled with love, beauty and kindness? Or do you sometimes wonder why God loves you?

You can only see the real you through the eyes of truth if you truly know Jesus. And the more you know Him and experience Him in your life, the more you will realize how special you are. The love of your Savior places you in perfect beauty before the Father's throne.

To really comprehend God's all-encompassing and unconditional love for us takes time. It is a lifelong journey with Him. It is a process in which we continually seek Him in order to grow step by step in the knowledge and understanding of His loving character.

And the closer we get to Him, the better our understanding will be of the right Way, the Truth and Life. This will enable us to offer the Bread of life to others.

Forget who you are when you look in the mirror. Learn to see through the compassionate eyes of the Man who loves you more than His own life and then realize that through Him your soul is clothed in heavenly beauty. Beauty then sings:

"Dear child, God loves you infinitely!"

Lord Jesus,
when I look at myself,
I see only
human brokenness,
fallibility and imperfection.

Then I look into Your eyes
and I see love:
unconditional,
undeserved
and all-encompassing love!

Please place in my heart
some of that greatness in my heart
so that
I may mirror Your perfect love
to others.

*Amen.*

# God in You

Mothers look at their children through special eyes – not because their children are always so nice, clever or obedient, but because something of God's unconditional love, infinite kindness and ever-forgiving heart is instilled in them. And maybe also because a mother knows that her children are extensions of herself. Her children show the world what she looks like, how she lives and what she is like.

God looks at His children through more than special eyes; He looks at us through the blood of His Son and then declares: "You are Mine. Therefore, My love for you is perfect, irrespective of who or what you are.

"Believe, accept and experience it – and then be an extension of Me where you live every day. Yes, you have to go out and be Me."

I pray that from His glorious, unlimited
resources He will empower you
with inner strength through
His Spirit. Then Christ will
make His home in your hearts
as you trust in Him. Your roots
will grow down into God's love
and keep you strong.

Eph. 3:16-17

Remain in Jesus and His love ...

... and He
will remain
in you.